11·90

M.

I

THE Stars

LIGHTS IN THE NIGHT SKY

An Earlybird Book
by Jeanne Bendick

Illustrated by Chris Forsey

THE MILLBROOK PRESS INC.

BROOKFIELD, CONNECTICUT

Cataloging-in-Publication Data

Bendick, Jeanne
Stars, lights in the night sky.
Brookfield, CT, Millbrook Press, 1991.
32 p.; ill.: (Early Bird)
Includes index
ISBN 1-878841-00-9   523.8   BEN
1. Stars   2. Astronomy   3. Galaxies.

Published by The Millbrook Press Inc, 2 Old New Milford Road, Brookfield,
Connecticut 06804, USA

Produced by Eagle Books Limited, Vigilant House, 120 Wilton Road,
London SW1V 1JZ, England

Contents

The Stars

What do you see when you look up at the night
sky? You can see hundreds, maybe thousands, of
stars out there. But that's only a few of all the stars
there are. There may be more stars than there are
drops of water in all the oceans of the Earth.

4

You can see planets, too, in the night sky. We live on a planet – **Planet Earth.** Do you know how to tell planets from stars? Stars twinkle. Planets don't.

The stars look like tiny pinpoints of light. That's because they are so far away. Stars are very big.

5

One star looks much bigger to us than the other stars do, because it is much nearer. It's the star you see in the daytime.

We call that star the **Sun.**

Did you know that the Sun is a star?

What Are Stars?

Stars are made of burning gases.
They are hotter than anything you can picture.
They are hotter than firecrackers or furnaces.
They are hotter than volcanoes.
Stars shine with energy they make themselves.
The energy we can see that comes from our own star is called **sunlight.** We can also feel the Sun's energy as warmth.
The starlight you see at night is energy from those faraway stars.

Seeing Across Space

You don't actually see the stars themselves. They are too far away. What you see is the light each star gives off as it burns. The light has moved across space from the star to your eyes.

Distances in space are very big. The light from a star you see now may have left the star hundreds or thousands of years ago.

The light from another star might have left it when the dinosaurs lived on Earth.

And yet another star may be so far away that its light began to travel across space before there were any animals here at all. Stars this far away cannot usually be seen by themselves. We see them as part of a group of stars, their light all blended together.

Light left this star when airplanes were invented.

Light left this star when there were knights in armor.

Light left this star when there were dinosaurs.

Light left this star when the Earth was new.

Are All Stars Alike?

From Earth, most stars look alike. But they are not alike. Some stars are much, much brighter than our Sun.

Over half of all stars are pairs. They go together, like two shoes. These star neighbors swing around each other.

Some stars grow brighter and dimmer, brighter and dimmer. They are like lighthouses in space, each one flashing its own special signal, the way a lighthouse does.

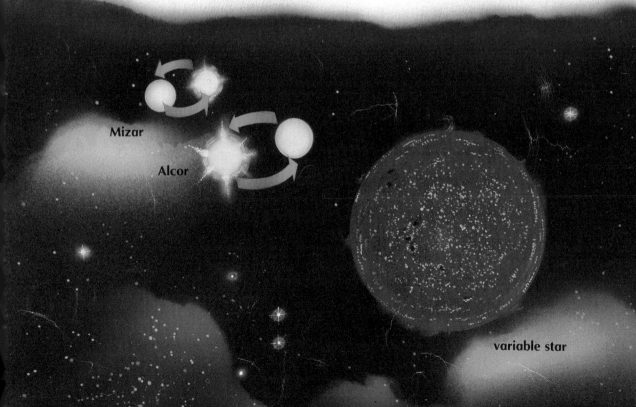

Mizar

Alcor

variable star

Some stars are called **novas.** They blaze up suddenly. For a few days, they are thousands of times brighter than before. Then they settle down again, though it may take years for them to return to normal. Novas may blaze up more than once.

Nova

Some giant stars are lighter than air. They would float on water.

Cooler, **white dwarf** stars are very, very dense. The stuff they are made of is so packed and jammed together that a spoonful of it might weigh more than a hundred elephants.

Arcturus is a red giant

Antares is a super-red giant star

The Sun is a middle-sized yellow star

Spica is a big, blue star

Proxima Centauri

Stars come in different sizes, too.
White dwarfs are no bigger than some planets.
Red giants are enormous. The red star
Betelgeuse (you can call it *Beetle Juice)* is a
supergiant. It is 400 million miles across.

Our Sun is a middle-sized star. Next to a red
giant, it would look like a green pea next to a
watermelon.

13

Where Do Stars Come From?

Stars are born.

Astronomers – scientists who study the stars – think that it takes millions of years for a star to be born.

A star begins as a huge cloud of dust and gas. Slowly, the dust and gas come together until the matter is packed so tightly that it begins to heat up. It gets hotter and hotter. At last it begins to burn. The star is born.

Young stars are big and pale red-orange in color.

Stars are born in the
star clouds called nebulae.

SPICA	SIRIUS	PROCYON	SUN	ARCTURUS	BETELGEUSE
Blue White	White	Green Yellow	Yellow	Orange	Red
HOTTEST					COOLEST

Do Stars Change?

As they get older, stars get smaller and hotter.
   They change color. Some become yellow. Our
Sun is a yellow star.
   White stars are hotter.
   Blue stars are the hottest.
   Star colors tell astronomers how hot a star is.

15

Stars change over billions of years. They use up the fuel that kept them burning.

When they start to cool, they spread out. The star swells like a balloon does when you blow it up. It becomes a red giant.

Betelgeuse

How Do Most Stars Die?

When its fuel is almost gone, a red giant falls in on itself. It shrinks and becomes a cold white dwarf, which is different from a hot white star.

At the end, it is a **black dwarf** star, with no heat and no light. Many stars die that way.

white dwarf

Star Explosions

Other, much bigger stars die faster. A very big star might explode in a super bright flash called a **supernova.**

A supernova sends out as much energy in a few seconds as our Sun does in a million years.

After the explosion, the supernova becomes a huge cloud of gas that spins around a very small, very heavy mass called a **neutron star.**

Neutron stars do not burn like other stars. However, some neutron stars send out beams of energy something like signals that come from radio stations on Earth. Stars like that are called **pulsars,** or radio stars.

Holes in Space

Some stars shrink even further. They become so dense that their **gravity** pulls everything around them into themselves. Gravity is a force that pulls on everything. Earth's gravity keeps you from drifting off into space.

black hole

The gravity of a huge, collapsed star can become so strong that not even light can get away. The star swallows everything around it.

Astronomers call these starlike objects **black holes.**

Black holes are very mysterious. Time and space inside a black hole may be quite different from how we know it.

Astronomers aren't even sure they have found a black hole yet.

Aquarius

Pictures in the Sky

A long time ago, people gave names to the brightest stars. They also gave names to the groups of stars that seemed to stay together as they moved across the night sky.

24

Leo

Cancer

Gemini

Orion

Pegasus

Great Bear

We call these star groups **constellations.**
The stars in constellations aren't really together
at all. They only look that way. People saw in
them pictures of imaginary beings, objects, and
animals.

Crowds of Stars

Constellations are fun, but they aren't real. Some groups of stars, however, really do go together.

A great many stars travel together in clusters for as long as they live. Star clusters are like clouds of stars.

A huge round ball of stars is called a **globular cluster.**

The stars in an **open cluster** are farther apart, and the cloud has no real shape.

The Big Star Clusters

Really big star clusters are called **galaxies.**
   There are billions of stars in a galaxy.
   Galaxies have different shapes.
   Some galaxies are spirals, which look like pinwheels.
   Some are round.
   Some are shaped like footballs.
   Some have no shape at all that we can recognize.

spiral galaxy

round galaxy

elliptical galaxy

Our own galaxy, the **Milky Way,** seems to be a big spiral with arms, rolling through space.

Our star and its planets and moons together are called the **Solar System.** The Solar System is out near the edge of the Milky Way Galaxy.

Astronomers once thought that our galaxy was the whole universe. Now we know that there are even more galaxies than all the single stars you can see in the night sky.

Milky Way

Index